The Collection and The Lover

The Collection, a Associated Rediffu by the Royal Sha Aldwych Theatre the main themes work: menace and <u>lack of communication.</u> *The Lover* is a one-act play for television, in which two characters play the double parts of husband-lover and wife-mistress. Also included is a short story, *The Examination*.

THE COLLECTION
and
THE LOVER

BY

Harold Pinter

LONDON

METHUEN & CO LTD

11 NEW FETTER LANE EC4

First published 1963
Second edition 1964
SBN 416 26750 5
2 . 1
Paperback edition first published 1966
Reprinted 1968
SBN 416 63210 6
1 . 2
© *1963 by H. Pinter Ltd*
Printed and bound in Great Britain by
W & J Mackay & Co Ltd
Chatham

Contents

My thanks are due to the editor of PROSPECT, in which 'The Examination' first appeared.   H.P.

TO VIVIEN

AND

PETER WILLES

The Collection

THE COLLECTION was first presented by Associated Rediffusion Television, London, on 11 May, 1961, with the following cast:

HARRY, *a man in his forties*	Griffith Jones
JAMES, *a man in his thirties*	Anthony Bate
STELLA, *a woman in her thirties*	Vivien Merchant
BILL, *a man in his late twenties*	John Ronane

Directed by Joan Kemp-Welch

The play was first presented on the stage at the Aldwych Theatre on 18 June 1962, with the following cast:

HARRY	Michael Hordern
JAMES	Kenneth Haigh
STELLA	Barbara Murray
BILL	John Ronane

Directed by Peter Hall and Harold Pinter

AUTUMN

The stage is divided into three areas, two peninsulas and a promontory. Each area is distinct and separate from the other.

Stage left, HARRY'S house in Belgravia. Elegant décor. Period furnishing. This set comprises the living-room, hall, front door and staircase to first floor. Kitchen exit below staircase.

Stage right, JAMES'S flat in Chelsea. Tasteful contemporary furnishing. This set comprises the living-room only. Offstage right, other rooms and front door.

Upstage centre on promontory, telephone box.

The telephone box is lit in a half light. A figure can be dimly observed inside it, with his back to the audience. The rest of the stage is dark. In the house the telephone is ringing. It is late at night.

Night light in house fades up. Street fades up.

HARRY *approaches the house, opens the front door and goes in. He switches on a light in the hall, goes into the living-room, walks to the telephone and lifts it.*

HARRY. Hullo.
VOICE. Is that you, Bill?
HARRY. No, he's in bed. Who's this?
VOICE. In bed?
HARRY. Who is this?
VOICE. What's he doing in bed?

    Pause.

HARRY. Do you know it's four o'clock in the morning?
VOICE. Well, give him a nudge. Tell him I want a word with him. (*Pause.*)
HARRY. Who is this?
VOICE. Go and wake him up, there's a good boy. (*Pause.*)
HARRY. Are you a friend of his?
VOICE. He'll know me when he sees me.
HARRY. Oh yes?

    Pause.

VOICE. Aren't you going to wake him?
HARRY. No, I'm not.

    Pause.

VOICE. Tell him I'll be in touch.

The telephone cuts off. HARRY *replaces the receiver and stands still. The figure leaves the telephone box.* HARRY *walks slowly into the hall and up the stairs.*
Fade to blackout.
Fade up on flat. It is morning.
JAMES, *smoking, enters and sits on the sofa.*
STELLA *enters from a bedroom fixing a bracelet on her wrist. She goes to the cabinet, takes a perfume atomizer from her handbag and uses it on her throat and hands. She puts the atomizer into her bag and begins to put her gloves on.*

STELLA. I'm going.

Pause.

Aren't you coming in today?

Pause.

JAMES. No.
STELLA. You had to meet those people from . . .

Pause. She slowly walks to an armchair, picks up her jacket and puts it on.

You had to meet those people about that order. Shall I phone them when I get to the shop?
JAMES. You could do . . . yes.
STELLA. What are you going to do?

He looks at her, with a brief smile, then away.

Jimmy . . .

Pause.

Are you going out?

Pause.

Will you . . . be in tonight?

JAMES *reaches for a glass ashtray, flicks ash, and regards*

the ashtray. STELLA *turns and leaves the room. The front
door slams.* JAMES *continues regarding the ashtray.*
Fade to half light.
Fade up on house. Morning.
BILL *brings on a tray from the kitchen and places it on the
table, arranges it, pours tea, sits, picks up a newspaper, reads,
drinks.* HARRY, *in a dressing-gown, descends the stairs, trips,
stumbles.*

BILL (*turning*). What have you done?
HARRY. I tripped on that stair rod!

He comes into the room.

BILL. All right.
HARRY. It's that stair rod. I thought you said you were going
to fix it.
BILL. I did fix it.
HARRY. Well, you didn't fix it very well.

He sits, holding his head.

Ooh.

BILL *pours tea for him.*
In the flat, JAMES *stubs his cigarette and goes out. The
lights in the flat fade out.*
HARRY *sips the tea, then puts the cup down.*

Where's my fruit juice? I haven't had my fruit juice.

BILL *regards the fruit juice on the tray.*

What's it doing over there?

BILL *gives it to him.* HARRY *sips it.*

What's this? Pineapple?

BILL. Grapefruit.

Pause.

HARRY. I'm sick and tired of that stair rod. Why don't you screw it in or something? You're supposed . . . you're supposed to be able to use your hands.

Pause.

BILL. What time did you get in?
HARRY. Four.
BILL. Good party?

Pause.

HARRY. You didn't make any toast this morning.
BILL. No. Do you want some?
HARRY. No. I don't.
BILL. I can if you like.
HARRY. It's all right. Don't bother.

Pause.

How are you spending your day today?
BILL. Go and see a film, I think.
HARRY. Wonderful life you lead. (*Pause.*) Do you know some maniac telephoned you last night?

BILL *looks at him.*

Just as I got in. Four o'clock. Walked in the door and the telephone was ringing.
BILL. Who was it?
HARRY. I've no idea.
BILL. What did he want?
HARRY. You. He was shy, wouldn't tell me his name.
BILL. Huh.

Pause.

HARRY. Who could it have been?
BILL. I've no idea.
HARRY. He was very insistent. Said he was going to get in touch again. (*Pause.*) Who the hell was it?

BILL. I've just said . . . I haven't the remotest idea.

Pause.

HARRY. Did you meet anyone last week?
BILL. Meet anyone? What do you mean?
HARRY. I mean could it have been anyone you met? You must have met lots of people.
BILL. I didn't speak to a soul.
HARRY. Must have been miserable for you.
BILL. I was only there one night, wasn't I? Some more?
HARRY. No, thank you.

> BILL *pours tea for himself.*
> *The telephone box fades up to half light, disclosing a figure entering it.*

I must shave.

> HARRY *sits, looking at* BILL, *who is reading the paper After a moment* BILL *looks up.*

BILL. Mmnnn?

> *Silence.* HARRY *stands, leaves the room and exits up the stairs, treading carefully over the stair rod.* BILL *reads the paper. The telephone rings.*
> BILL *lifts the receiver.*

Hullo.
VOICE. Is that you, Bill?
BILL. Yes?
VOICE. Are you in?
BILL. Who's this?
VOICE. Don't move. I'll be straight round.
BILL. What do you mean? Who is this?
VOICE. About two minutes. All right?
BILL. You can't do that. I've got some people here.
VOICE. Never mind. We can go into another room.

BILL. This is ridiculous. Do I know you?

VOICE. You'll know me when you see me.

BILL. Do you know me?

VOICE. Just stay where you are. I'll be right round.

BILL. But what do you want, who – ? You can't do that. I'm going straight out. I won't be in.

VOICE. See you.

The phone cuts off. BILL *replaces the receiver.*
The lights on the telephone box fade as the figure comes out and exits left.
BILL *puts on his jacket, goes into the hall, puts on his overcoat, swift but not hurried, opens the front door, and goes out. He exits up right.* HARRY'S *voice from upstairs.*

HARRY. Bill, was that you?

He appears at the head of the stairs.

Bill!

He goes downstairs, into the living-room, stands, observes the tray, and takes the tray into the kitchen.
JAMES *comes from up left in the street and looks at the house.*
HARRY *comes out of the kitchen, goes into the hall and up the stairs.*
JAMES *rings the bell.*
HARRY *comes down the stairs and opens the door.*

Yes?

JAMES. I'm looking for Bill Lloyd.

HARRY. He's out. Can I help?

JAMES. When will he be in?

HARRY. I can't say. Does he know you?

JAMES. I'll try some other time then.

HARRY. Well, perhaps you'd like to leave your name. I can tell him when I see him.

JAMES. No, that's all right. Just tell him I called.

HARRY. Tell him who called?

JAMES. Sorry to bother you.

HARRY. Just a minute. (JAMES *turns back*.) You're not the man who telephoned last night, are you?

JAMES. Last night?

HARRY. You didn't telephone early this morning?

JAMES. No . . . sorry . . .

HARRY. Well, what do you want?

JAMES. I'm looking for Bill.

HARRY. You didn't by any chance telephone just now?

JAMES. I think you've got the wrong man.

HARRY. I think you have.

JAMES. I don't think you know anything about it.

> JAMES *turns and goes.* HARRY *stands watching him.*
> *Fade to blackout.*
> *Fade up moonlight in flat.*
> *The front door closes, in flat.*
> STELLA *comes in, stands, switches on a lamp. She turns in the direction of the other rooms.*

STELLA. Jimmy?

> *Silence.*
> *She takes her gloves off, puts her handbag down, and is still. She goes to the record player, and puts on a record. It is 'Charlie Parker'. She listens, then exists to the bedroom. Fade up house. Night.*
> BILL *enters the living-room from the kitchen with magazines. He throws them in the hearth, goes to the drinks table and pours a drink, then lies on the floor with a drink by the hearth, flicking through a magazine.* STELLA *comes back into the room with a white Persian kitten. She lies back on the sofa, nuzzling it.* HARRY *comes downstairs, glances in at* BILL, *exits and walks down the street to up right.* JAMES *appears at the front door of the house from up left, looks after*

HARRY, *and rings the bell.* BILL *stands, and goes to the door.*
Fade flat to half light and music out.

BILL. Yes?

JAMES. Bill Lloyd?

BILL. Yes?

JAMES. Oh, I'd . . . I'd like to have a word with you.

Pause.

BILL. I'm sorry, I don't think I know you?

JAMES. Don't you?

BILL. No.

JAMES. Well, there's something I'd like to talk to you about

BILL. I'm terribly sorry, I'm busy.

JAMES. It won't take long.

BILL. I'm awfully sorry. Perhaps you'd like to put it down on paper and send it to me.

JAMES. That's not possible.

Pause.

BILL (*closing door*). Do forgive me –

JAMES (*foot in door*). Look. I want to speak to you.

Pause.

BILL. Did you phone me today?

JAMES. That's right. I called, but you'd gone out.

BILL. You called here? I didn't know that.

JAMES. I think I'd better come in, don't you?

BILL. You can't just barge into someone's house like this, you know. What do you want?

JAMES. Why don't you stop wasting your time and let me in?

BILL. I could call the police.

JAMES. Not worth it.

They stare at each other.

BILL. All right.

> JAMES *goes in.* BILL *closes the door.* JAMES *goes through the hall and into the living-room.* BILL *follows.* JAMES *looks about the room.*

JAMES. Got any olives?

BILL. How did you know my name?

JAMES. No olives?

BILL. Olives? I'm afraid not.

JAMES. You mean to say you don't keep olives for your guests?

BILL. You're not my guest, you're an intruder. What can I do for you?

JAMES. Do you mind if I sit down?

BILL. Yes, I do.

JAMES. You'll get over it.

> JAMES *sits.* BILL *stands.* JAMES *stands, takes off his overcoat, throws it on an armchair, and sits again.*

BILL. What's your name, old boy?

> JAMES *reaches to a bowl of fruit and breaks off a grape, which he eats.*

JAMES. Where shall I put the pips?

BILL. In your wallet.

> JAMES *takes out his wallet and deposits the pips. He regards* BILL.

JAMES. You're not a bad-looking bloke.

BILL. Oh, thanks.

JAMES. You're not a film star, but you're quite tolerable looking, I suppose.

BILL. That's more than I can say for you.

JAMES. I'm not interested in what you can say for me.

BILL. To put it quite bluntly, old chap, I'm even less interested than you are. Now look, come on please, what do you want?

JAMES *stands, walks to the drinks table and stares at the bottles. In the flat,* STELLA *rises with the kitten and goes off slowly, nuzzling it. The flat fades to blackout.* JAMES *pours himself a whisky.*

Cheers.

JAMES. Did you have a good time in Leeds last week?

BILL. What?

JAMES. Did you have a good time in Leeds last week?

BILL. Leeds?

JAMES. Did you enjoy yourself?

BILL. What makes you think I was in Leeds.

JAMES. Tell me all about it. See much of the town? Get out to the country at all?

BILL. What are you talking about?

Pause.

JAMES (*with fatigue*). Aaah. You were down there for the dress collection. You took some of your models.

BILL. Did I?

JAMES. You stayed at the Westbury Hotel.

BILL. Oh?

JAMES. Room 142.

BILL. 142? Oh. Was it comfortable?

JAMES. Comfortable enough.

BILL. Oh, good.

JAMES. Well, you had your yellow pyjamas with you.

BILL. Did I really? What, the ones with the black initials?

JAMES. Yes, you had them on you in 165.

BILL. In what?

JAMES. 165.

BILL. 165? I thought I was in 142.

JAMES. You booked into 142. But you didn't stay there.

BILL. Well, that's a bit silly, isn't it? Booking a room and not staying in it?

JAMES. 165 is just along the passage to 142; you're not far away.

BILL. Oh well, that's a relief.

JAMES. You could easily nip back to shave.

BILL. From 165?

JAMES. Yes.

BILL. What was I doing there?

JAMES (*casually*). My wife was in there. That's where you slept with her.

    Silence.

BILL. Well . . . who told you that?

JAMES. She did.

BILL. You should have her seen to.

JAMES. Be careful.

BILL. Mmmm? Who is your wife?

JAMES. You know her.

BILL. I don't think so.

JAMES. No?

BILL. No, I don't think so at all.

JAMES. I see.

BILL. I was nowhere near Leeds last week, old chap. Nowhere near your wife either, I'm quite sure of that. Apart from that, I . . . just don't do such things. Not in my book.

    Pause.

I wouldn't dream of it. Well, I think that closes that subject, don't you?

JAMES. Come here. I want to tell you something.

BILL. I'm expecting guests in a minute, you know. Cocktails, I'm standing for Parliament next season.

JAMES. Come here.

BILL. I'm going to be Minister for Home Affairs.

    JAMES *moves to him.*

JAMES (*confidentially*). When you treat my wife like a whore, then I think I'm entitled to know what you've got to say about it.

BILL. But I don't know your wife.

JAMES. You do. You met her at ten o'clock last Friday in the lounge. You fell into conversation, you bought her a couple of drinks, you went upstairs together in the lift. In the lift you never took your eyes from her, you found you were both on the same floor, you helped her out, by her arm. You stood with her in the corridor, looking at her. You touched her shoulder, said good night, went to your room, she went to hers, you changed into your yellow pyjamas and black dressing-gown, you went down the passage and knocked on her door, you'd left your toothpaste in town. She opened the door, you went in, she was still dressed. You admired the room, it was so feminine, you felt awake, didn't feel like sleeping, you sat down, on the bed. She wanted you to go, you wouldn't. She became upset, you sympathized, away from home, on a business trip, horrible life, especially for a woman, you comforted her, you gave her solace, you stayed.

> *Pause.*

BILL. Look, do you mind . . . just going off now. You're giving me a bit of a headache.

JAMES. You knew she was married . . . why did you feel it necessary . . . to do that?

BILL. She must have known she was married, too. Why did she feel it necessary . . . to do that?

> *Pause.*

(*With a chuckle.*) That's got you, hasn't it?

> *Pause.*

Well, look, it's really just a lot of rubbish. You know that.

> BILL *goes to the cigarette box and lights a cigarette.*

Is she supposed to have resisted me at all?

JAMES. A little.

BILL. Only a little?

JAMES. Yes.

BILL. Do you believe her?

JAMES. Yes.

BILL. Everything she says?

JAMES. Sure.

BILL. Did she bite at all?

JAMES. No.

BILL. Scratch?

JAMES. A little.

BILL. You've got a devoted wife, haven't you? Keeps you well informed, right up to the minutest detail. She scratched a little, did she? Where? (*Holds up a hand.*) On the hand? No scar. No scar anywhere. Absolutely unscarred. We can go before a commissioner of oaths, if you like. I'll strip, show you my unscarred body. Yes, what we need is an independent witness. You got any chambermaids on your side or anything?

JAMES *applauds briefly.*

JAMES. You're a wag, aren't you? I never thought you'd be such a wag. You've really got a sense of fun. You know what I'd call you?

BILL. What?

JAMES. A wag.

BILL. Oh, thanks very much.

JAMES. No, I'm glad to pay a compliment when a compliment's due. What about a drink?

BILL. That's good of you.

JAMES. What will you have?

BILL. Got any vodka?

JAMES. Let's see. Yes, I think we can find you some vodka.

BILL. Oh, scrumptious.

JAMES. Say that again.

BILL. What?

JAMES. That word.

BILL. What, scrumptious?

JAMES. That's it.

BILL. Scrumptious.

JAMES. Marvellous. You probably remember that from school, don't you?

BILL. Now that you mention it I think you might be right.

JAMES. I thought I was. Here's your vodka.

BILL. That's very generous of you.

JAMES. Not at all. Cheers. (*They drink.*)

BILL. Cheers.

JAMES. Eh, come here.

BILL. What?

JAMES. I bet you're a wow at parties.

BILL. Well, it's nice of you to say so, but I wouldn't say I was all that much of a wow.

JAMES. Go on, I bet you are. (*Pause.*)

BILL. You think I'm a wow, do you?

JAMES. At parties I should think you are.

BILL. No, I'm not much of a wow really. The bloke I share this house with is, though.

JAMES. Oh, I met him. Looked a jolly kind of chap.

BILL. Yes, he's very good at parties. Bit of a conjurer.

JAMES. What, rabbits?

BILL. Well, not so much rabbits, no.

JAMES. No rabbits?

BILL. No. He doesn't like rabbits, actually. They give him hay fever.

JAMES. Poor chap.

BILL. Yes, it's a pity.

JAMES. Seen a doctor about it?

BILL. Oh, he's had it since he was that high.

JAMES. Brought up in the country, I suppose?

BILL. In a manner of speaking, yes.

Pause.

Ah well, it's been very nice meeting you, old chap. You must come again when the weather's better.

JAMES *makes a sudden move forward.* BILL *starts back, and falls over a pouffe on to the floor.* JAMES *chuckles. Pause.*

You've made me spill my drink. You've made me spill it on my cardigan.

JAMES *stands over him.*

I could easily kick you from here.

Pause.

Are you going to let me get up?

Pause.

Are you going to let me get up?

Pause.

Now listen . . . I'll tell you what . . .

Pause.

If you let me get up . . .

Pause.

I'm not very comfortable.

Pause.

If you let me get up . . . I'll . . . I'll tell you . . . the truth . . .

Pause.

JAMES. Tell me the truth from there.
BILL. No. No, when I'm up.

JAMES. Tell me from there.

Pause.

BILL. Oh well. I'm only telling you because I'm utterly bored
. . . The truth . . . is that it never happened . . . what you
said, anyway. I didn't know she was married. She never
told me. Never said a word. But nothing of that . . . happened, I can assure you. All that happened was . . . you
were right, actually, about going up in the lift . . . we . . .
got out of the lift, and then suddenly she was in my arms.
Really wasn't my fault, nothing was further from my mind,
biggest surprise of my life, must have found me terribly
attractive quite suddenly, I don't know . . . but I . . . I
didn't refuse. Anyway, we just kissed a bit, only a few
minutes, by the lift, no one about, and that was that – she
went to her room.

He props himself up on the pouffe.

The rest of it just didn't happen. I mean, I wouldn't do
that sort of thing. I mean, that sort of thing . . . it's just
meaningless. I can understand that you're upset, of course,
but honestly, there was nothing else to it. Just a few kisses.
(BILL *rises, wiping his cardigan.*) I'm dreadfully sorry, really,
I mean, I've no idea why she should make up all that.
Pure fantasy. Really rather naughty of her. Rather alarming.
(*Pause.*) Do you know her well?

JAMES. And then about midnight you went into her private
bathroom and had a bath. You sang 'Coming through the
Rye'. You used her bath towel. Then you walked about the
room with her bath towel, pretending you were a Roman.

BILL. Did I?

JAMES. Then I phoned.

Pause.

I spoke to her. Asked her how she was. She said she was

all right. Her voice was a little low. I asked her to speak up. She didn't have much to say. You were sitting on the bed, next to her.

Silence.

BILL. Not sitting. Lying.

Blackout.
Church bells.
Full light up on both the flat and the house.
Sunday morning.
JAMES *is sitting alone in the living-room of the flat, reading the paper.* HARRY *and* BILL *are sitting in the living-room of the house, coffee before them.* BILL *is reading the paper.*
HARRY *is watching him.*
Silence.
Church bells.
Silence.

HARRY. Put that paper down.
BILL. What?
HARRY. Put it down.
BILL. Why?
HARRY. You've read it.
BILL. No, I haven't. There's lots to read, you know.
HARRY. I told you to put it down.

BILL *looks at him, throws the paper at him coolly and rises.*
HARRY *picks it up and reads.*

BILL. Oh, you just wanted it yourself, did you?
HARRY. Want it? I don't want it.

HARRY *crumples the paper deliberately and drops it.*

I don't want it. Do you want it?
BILL. You're being a little erratic this morning, aren't you?

HARRY. Am I?

BILL. I would say you were.

HARRY. Well, you know what it is, don't you?

BILL. No.

HARRY. It's the church bells. You know how church bells always set me off. You know how they affect me.

BILL. I never hear them.

HARRY. You're not the sort of person who would, are you?

BILL. I'm finding all this faintly idiotic.

BILL *bends to pick up the paper.*

HARRY. Don't touch that paper.

BILL. Why not?

HARRY. Don't touch it.

BILL *stares at him and then slowly picks it up.*
Silence.
He tosses it to HARRY.

BILL. You have it. I don't want it.

BILL *goes out and up the stairs.* HARRY *opens the paper and reads it.*
In the flat, STELLA *comes in with a tray of coffee and biscuits. She places the tray on the coffee-table and passes a cup to* JAMES. *She sips.*

STELLA. Would you like a biscuit?

JAMES. No, thank you.

Pause.

STELLA. I'm going to have one.

JAMES. You'll get fat.

STELLA. From biscuits?

JAMES. You don't want to get fat, do you?

STELLA. Why not?

JAMES. Perhaps you do.

STELLA. It's not one of my aims.
JAMES. What is your aim?

Pause.

I'd like an olive.
STELLA. Olive? We haven't got any.
JAMES. How do you know?
STELLA. I know.
JAMES. Have you looked?
STELLA. I don't need to look, do I? I know what I've got.
JAMES. You know what you've got?

Pause.

Why haven't we got any olives?
STELLA. I didn't know you liked them.
JAMES. That must be the reason why we've never had them
in the house. You've simply never been interested enough
in olives to ask whether I liked them or not.

The telephone rings in the house. HARRY *puts the paper
down and goes to it.* BILL *comes down the stairs. They stop,
facing each other, momentarily.* HARRY *lifts the receiver.*
BILL *walks into the room, picks up the paper and sits.*

HARRY. Hullo. What? No. Wrong number. (*Replaces receiver.*)
Wrong number. Who do you think it was?
BILL. I didn't think.
HARRY. Oh, by the way, a chap called for you yesterday.
BILL. Oh yes?
HARRY. Just after you'd gone out.
BILL. Oh yes?
HARRY. Ah well, time for the joint. Roast or chips?
BILL. I don't want any potatoes, thank you.
HARRY. No potatoes? What an extraordinary thing. Yes, this
chap, he was asking for you, he wanted you.
BILL. What for?

HARRY. He wanted to know if you ever cleaned your shoes
with furniture polish.

BILL. Really? How odd.

HARRY. Not odd. Some kind of national survey.

BILL. What did he look like?

HARRY. Oh . . . lemon hair, nigger brown teeth, wooden leg,
bottlegreen eyes and a toupee. Know him?

BILL. Never met him.

HARRY. You'd know him if you saw him.

BILL. I doubt it.

HARRY. What, a man who looked like that?

BILL. Plenty of men look like that.

HARRY. That's true. That's very true. The only thing is that
this particular man was here last night.

BILL. Was he? I didn't see him.

HARRY. Oh yes, he was here, but I've got a funny feeling he
wore a mask. It was the same man, but he wore a mask,
that's all there is to it. He didn't dance here last night, did
he, or do any gymnastics?

BILL. No one danced here last night.

HARRY. Aah. Well, that's why you didn't notice his wooden
leg. I couldn't help seeing it myself when he came to the
front door because he stood on the top step stark naked.
Didn't seem very cold, though. He had a waterbottle under
his arm instead of a hat.

BILL. Those church bells have certainly left their mark on
you.

HARRY. They haven't helped, but the fact of the matter is,
old chap, that I don't like strangers coming into my house
without an invitation. (*Pause.*) Who is this man and what
does he want?

Pause. BILL *rises.*

BILL. Will you excuse me? I really think it's about time I was
dressed, don't you?

BILL *goes up the stairs.*
HARRY, *after a moment, turns and follows. He slowly ascends the stairs.*
Fade to blackout on house.
In the flat JAMES *is still reading the paper.* STELLA *is sitting silently.*
Silence.

STELLA. What do you think about going for a run today . . . in the country?

Pause. JAMES *puts the paper down.*

JAMES. I've come to a decision.
STELLA. What?
JAMES. I'm going to go and see him.
STELLA. See him? Who? (*Pause.*) What for?
JAMES. Oh . . . have a chat with him.
STELLA. What's the point of doing that?
JAMES. I feel I'd like to.
STELLA. I just don't see . . . what there is to be gained. What's the point of it?

Pause.

What are you going to do, hit him?
JAMES. No, no. I'd just like to hear what he's got to say.
STELLA. Why?
JAMES. I want to know what his attitude is.

Pause.

STELLA. He doesn't matter.
JAMES. What do you mean?
STELLA. He's not important.
JAMES. Do you mean anyone would have done? You mean it just happened to be him, but it might as well have been anyone?

STELLA. No.

JAMES. What then?

STELLA. Of course it couldn't have been anyone. It was him. It was just . . . something . . .

JAMES. That's what I mean. It was him. That's why I think he's worth having a look at. I want to see what he's like. It'll be instructive, educational.

Pause.

STELLA. Please don't go and see him. You don't know where he lives, anyway.

JAMES. You don't think I should see him?

STELLA. It won't . . . make you feel any better.

JAMES. I want to see if he's changed.

STELLA. What do you mean?

JAMES. I want to see if he's changed from when I last saw him. He may have gone down the drain since I last saw him. I must say he looked in good shape, though.

STELLA. You've never seen him.

Pause.

You don't know him.

Pause.

You don't know where he lives?

Pause.

When did you see him?

JAMES. We had dinner together last night.

STELLA. What?

JAMES. Splendid host.

STELLA. I don't believe it.

JAMES. Ever been to his place?

Pause.

Rather nice. Ever been there?

STELLA. I met him in Leeds, that's all.

JAMES. Oh, is that all. Well, we'll have to go round there one night. The grub's good, I can't deny it. I found him quite charming.

Pause.

He remembered the occasion well. He was perfectly frank. You know, a man's man. Straight from the shoulder. He entirely confirmed your story.

STELLA. Did he?

JAMES. Mmm. Only thing . . . he rather implied that you led him on. Typical masculine thing to say, of course.

STELLA. That's a lie.

JAMES. You know what men are. I reminded him that you'd resisted, and you'd hated the whole thing, but that you'd been – how can we say – somehow hypnotized by him, it happens sometimes. He agreed it can happen sometimes. He told me he'd been hypnotized once by a cat. Wouldn't go into any more details, though. Still, I must admit we rather hit it off. We've got the same interests. He was most amusing over the brandy.

STELLA. I'm not interested.

JAMES. In fact, he was most amusing over the whole thing.

STELLA. Was he?

JAMES. But especially over the brandy. He's got the right attitude, you see. As a man, I can only admire it.

STELLA. What is his attitude?

JAMES. What's your attitude?

STELLA. I don't know what you're . . . I just don't know what you're . . . I just . . . hoped you'd understand . . .

She covers her face, crying.

JAMES. Well, I do understand, but only after meeting him. Now I'm perfectly happy. I can see it both ways, three

ways, all ways . . . every way. It's perfectly clear, there's
nothing to it, everything's back to normal. The only difference is that I've come across a man I can respect. It isn't
often you can do that, that that happens, and really I suppose I've got you to thank.

He bends forward and pats her arm.

Thanks.

Pause.

He reminds me of a bloke I went to school with. Hawkins.
Honestly, he reminded me of Hawkins. Hawkins was an
opera fan, too. So's what's-his-name. I'm a bit of an opera
fan myself. Always kept it a dead secret. I might go along
with your bloke to the opera one night. He says he can always
get free seats. He knows quite a few of that crowd. Maybe I
can track old Hawkins down and take him along, too. He's
a very cultivated bloke, your bloke, quite a considerable
intelligence at work there, I thought. He's got a collection of
Chinese pots stuck on a wall, must have cost at least fifteen
hundred a piece. Well, you can't help noticing that sort of
thing. I mean, you couldn't say he wasn't a man of taste.
He's brimming over with it. Well, I suppose he must have
struck you the same way. No, really, I think I should thank
you, rather than anything else. After two years of marriage
it looks as though, by accident, you've opened up a whole
new world for me.

Fade to blackout.
Fade up house. Night.
BILL *comes in from the kitchen with a tray of olives, cheese,
crisps, and a transistor radio, playing Vivaldi, very quietly.
He puts the tray on the table, arranges the cushions and eats
a crisp.* JAMES *appears at the front door and rings the bell.*
BILL *goes to the door, opens it, amd* JAMES *comes in. In
the hall he helps* JAMES *off with his coat.*

JAMES *comes into the room,* BILL *follows.* JAMES *notices the tray with the olives, and smiles.* BILL *smiles.* JAMES *goes up to the Chinese vases and examines them.* BILL *pours drinks. In the flat the telephone rings.*
Fade up on flat. Night.
Fade up half light on telephone box.
A figure can be dimly seen in the telephone box. STELLA *enters from the bedroom, holding the kitten. She goes to the telephone.* BILL *gives* JAMES *a glass. They drink.*

STELLA. Hullo.
HARRY. Is that you, James?
STELLA. What? No, it isn't. Who's this?
HARRY. Where's James?
STELLA. He's out.
HARRY. Out? Oh, well, all right. I'll be straight round.
STELLA. What are you talking about? Who are you?
HARRY. Don't go out.

The telephone cuts off. STELLA *replaces the receiver and sits upright with the kitten on the chair.*
Fade to half light on flat.
Fade telephone box.

JAMES. You know something? You remind me of a chap I knew once. Hawkins. Yes. He was quite a tall lad.
BILL. Tall, was he?
JAMES. Yes.
BILL. Now why should I remind you of him?
JAMES. He was quite a card. (*Pause.*)
BILL. Tall, was he?
JAMES. That's . . . what he was.
BILL. Well, you're not short.
JAMES. I'm not tall.
BILL. Quite broad.
JAMES. That doesn't make me tall.

BILL. I never said it did.

JAMES. Well, what are you saying?

BILL. Nothing. (*Pause.*)

JAMES. I wouldn't exactly say I was broad, either.

BILL. Well, you only see yourself in the mirror, don't you?

JAMES. That's good enough for me.

BILL. They're deceptive.

JAMES. Mirrors?

BILL. Very.

JAMES. Have you got one?

BILL. What?

JAMES. A mirror.

BILL. There's one right in front of you.

JAMES. So there is.

> JAMES *looks into the mirror.*

Come here. You look in it, too.

> BILL *stands by him and looks. They look together, and then* JAMES *goes to the left of the mirror, and looks again at* BILL'S *reflection.*

I don't think mirrors are deceptive.

> JAMES *sits.* BILL *smiles, and turns up the radio. They sit listening.*
> *Fade to half light on house and radio out.*
> *Fade up full on flat.*
> *Doorbell.*
> STELLA *rises and goes off to the front door. The voices are heard off.*

STELLA. Yes?

HARRY. How do you do. My name's Harry Kane. I wonder if I might have a word with you. There's no need to be alarmed. May I come in?

STELLA. Yes.

HARRY (*entering*). In here?
STELLA. Yes.

> *They come into the room.*

HARRY. What a beautiful lamp.
STELLA. What can I do for you?
HARRY. Do you know Bill Lloyd?
STELLA. No.
HARRY. Oh, you don't?
STELLA. No.
HARRY. You don't know him personally?
STELLA. I don't, no.
HARRY. I found him in a slum, you know, by accident. Just happened to be in a slum one day and there he was. I realized he had talent straight away. I gave him a roof, gave him a job, and he came up trumps. We've been close friends for years.
STELLA. Oh yes?
HARRY. You know of him, of course, don't you, by repute? He's a dress designer.
STELLA. I know of him.
HARRY. You're both dress designers.
STELLA. Yes.
HARRY. You don't belong to the Rags and Bags Club, do you?
STELLA. The what?
HARRY. The Rags and Bags Club. I thought I might have seen you down there.
STELLA. No, I don't know it.
HARRY. Shame. You'd like it.

> *Pause.*

Yes.

> *Pause.*

I've come about your husband.

STELLA. Oh?

HARRY. Yes. He's been bothering Bill recently, with some fantastic story.

STELLA. I know about it. I'm very sorry.

HARRY. Oh, you know? Well, it's really been rather disturbing. I mean, the boy has his work to get on with. This sort of thing spoils his concentration.

STELLA. I'm sorry. It's . . . very unfortunate.

HARRY. It is.

Pause.

STELLA. I can't understand it . . . We've been happily married for two years, you see. I've . . . been away before, you know . . . showing dresses, here and there, my husband runs the business. But it's never happened before.

HARRY. What hasn't?

STELLA. Well, that my husband has suddenly dreamed up such a fantastic story, for no reason at all.

HARRY. That's what I said it was. I said it was a fantastic story.

STELLA. It is.

HARRY. That's what I said and that's what Bill says. We both think it's a fantastic story.

STELLA. I mean, Mr. Lloyd was in Leeds, but I hardly saw him, even though we were staying in the same hotel. I never met him or spoke to him . . . and then my husband suddenly accused me of . . . it's really been very distressing.

HARRY. Yes. What do you think the answer is? Do you think your husband . . . doesn't trust you, or something?

STELLA. Of course he does – he's just not been very well lately, actually . . . overwork.

HARRY. That's bad. Still, you know what it's like in our business. Why don't you take him on a long holiday? South of France.

STELLA. Yes. I'm very sorry that Mr. Lloyd has had to put up with all this, anyway.

HARRY. Oh, what a beautiful kitten, what a really beautiful kitten. Kitty, kitty, kitty, what do you call her, come here, kitty, kitty.

> HARRY *sits next to* STELLA *and proceeds to pet and nuzzle the kitten.*
> *Fade flat to half light.*
> *Fade up full on house.*
> BILL *and* JAMES, *with drinks in the same position.*
> *Music comes up.* BILL *turns off the radio.*
> *Music out.*

BILL. Hungry?
JAMES. No.
BILL. Biscuit?
JAMES. I'm not hungry.
BILL. I've got some olives.
JAMES. Really?
BILL. Like one?
JAMES. No, thanks.
BILL. Why not?
JAMES. I don't like them.

> *Pause.*

BILL. Don't like olives?

> *Pause.*

What on earth have you got against olives?

> *Pause.*

JAMES. I detest them.
BILL. Really?
JAMES. It's the smell I hate.

> *Pause.*

BILL. Cheese? I've got a splendid cheese knife.

He picks up a cheese knife.

Look. Don't you think it's splendid?

JAMES. Is it sharp?

BILL. Try it. Hold the blade. It won't cut you. Not if you handle it properly. Not if you grasp it firmly up to the hilt.

> JAMES *does not touch the knife.*
> BILL *stands holding it.*
> *Lights in house remain.*
> *Fade up flat to full.*

HARRY (*standing*). Well, good-bye, I'm glad we've had our little chat.

STELLA. Yes.

HARRY. It's all quite clear now.

STELLA. I'm glad.

> *They move to the door.*

HARRY. Oh, Mr. Lloyd asked me if I would give you his best wishes . . . and sympathies.

> *He goes out. She stands still.*

Good-bye.

> *The front door closes.* STELLA *lies on the sofa with the kitten. She rests her head, is still.*
> *Fade flat to half light.*

BILL. What are you frightened of?

JAMES (*moving away*). What's that?

BILL. What?

JAMES. I thought it was thunder.

BILL (*to him*). Why are you frightened of holding this blade?

JAMES. I'm not frightened. I was just thinking of the thunder last week, when you and my wife were in Leeds.

BILL. Oh, not again, surely? I thought we'd left all that

behind. Surely we have? You're not still worried about that, are you?

JAMES. Oh no. Just nostalgia, that's all.

BILL. Surely the wound heals when you know the truth, doesn't it? I mean, when the truth is verified? I would have thought it did.

JAMES. Of course.

BILL. What's there left to think about? It's a thing regretted, never to be repeated. No past, no future. Do you see what I mean? You're a chap who's been married for two years, aren't you, happily? There's a bond of iron between you and your wife. It can't be corroded by a trivial thing like this. I've apologized, she's apologized. Honestly, what more can you want?

Pause. JAMES *looks at him.* BILL *smiles.* HARRY *appears at the front door, opens and closes it quietly, and remains in the hall, unnoticed by the others.*

JAMES. Nothing.

BILL. Every woman is bound to have an outburst of . . . wild sensuality at one time or another. That's the way I look at it, anyway. It's part of their nature. Even though it may be the kind of sensuality of which you yourself have never been the fortunate recipient. What? (*He laughs.*) That is a husband's fate, I suppose. Mind you, I think it's the system that's at fault, not you. Perhaps she'll never need to do it again, who knows.

JAMES *stands, goes to the fruit bowl, and picks up the fruit knife. He runs his finger along the blade.*

JAMES. This is fairly sharp.

BILL. What do you mean?

JAMES. Come on.

BILL. I beg your pardon?

JAMES. Come on. You've got that one. I've got this one.

BILL. What about it?

JAMES. I get a bit tired of words sometimes, don't you? Let's have a game. For fun.

BILL. What sort of game?

JAMES. Let's have a mock duel.

BILL. I don't want a mock duel, thank you.

JAMES. Of course you do. Come on. First one who's touched is a sissy.

BILL. This is all rather unsubtle, don't you think?

JAMES. Not in the least. Come on, into first position.

BILL. I thought we were friends.

JAMES. Of course we're friends. What on earth's the matter with you? I'm not going to kill you. It's just a game, that's all. We're playing a game. You're not windy, are you?

BILL. I think it's silly.

JAMES. I say, you're a bit of a spoilsport, aren't you?

BILL. I'm putting my knife down anyway.

JAMES. Well, I'll pick it up.

JAMES *does so and faces him with two knives.*

BILL. Now you've got two.

JAMES. I've got another one in my hip pocket.

Pause.

BILL. What do you do, swallow them?

JAMES. Do you?

Pause. They stare at each other.

(*Suddenly.*) Go on! Swallow it!

JAMES *throws a knife at* BILL'S *face.* BILL *throws up a hand to protect his face and catches the knife by the blade. It cuts his hand.*

BILL. Ow!

JAMES. Well caught! What's the matter?

He examines BILL'S *hand.*

Let's have a look. Ah yes. Now you've got a scar on your hand. You didn't have one before, did you?

HARRY *comes into the room.*

HARRY (*entering*). What have you done, nipped your hand? Let's have a look. (*To* JAMES.) Only a little nip, isn't it? It's his own fault for not ducking. I must have told him dozens of times, you know, that if someone throws a knife at you the silliest thing you can do is to catch it. You're bound to hurt yourself, unless it's made of rubber. The safest thing to do is duck. You're Mr. Horne?

JAMES. That's right.

HARRY. I'm so glad to meet you. My name's Harry Kane. Bill been looking after you all right? I asked him to see that you stayed until I got back. So glad you could spare the time. What are we drinking? Whisky? Let's fill you up. You and your wife run that little boutique down the road, don't you? Funny we've never met, living so close, all in the same trade, eh? Here you are. Got one, Bill? Where's your glass? This one? Here . . . you are. Oh, stop rubbing your hand, for goodness' sake. It's only a cheese knife. Well, Mr. Horne, all the very best. Here's wishing us all health, happiness and prosperity in the time to come, not forgetting your wife, of course. Healthy minds in healthy bodies. Cheers.

They drink.

By the way, I've just seen your wife. What a beautiful kitten she has. You should see it, Bill; it's all white. We had a very pleasant chat, your wife and I. Listen . . . old chap . . . can I be quite blunt with you?

JAMES. Of course.

HARRY. Your wife . . . you see . . . made a little tiny confession to me. I think I can use that word.

Pause.

BILL *is sucking his hand.*

What she confessed was . . . that she'd made the whole thing up. She'd made the whole damn thing up. For some odd reason of her own. They never met, you see, Bill and your wife; they never even spoke. This is what Bill says, and this is now what your wife admits. They had nothing whatever to do with each other; they don't know each other. Women are very strange. But I suppose you know more about that than I do; she's your wife. If I were you I'd go home and knock her over the head with a saucepan and tell her not to make up such stories again.

Pause.

JAMES. She made the whole thing up, eh?

HARRY. I'm afraid she did.

JAMES. I see. Well, thanks very much for telling me.

HARRY. I thought it would be clearer for you, coming from someone completely outside the whole matter.

JAMES. Yes. Thank you.

HARRY. Isn't that so, Bill?

BILL. Oh, quite so. I don't even know the woman. Wouldn't know her if I saw her. Pure fantasy.

JAMES. How's your hand?

BILL. Not bad.

JAMES. Isn't it strange that you confirmed the whole of her story?

BILL. It amused me to do so.

JAMES. Oh?

BILL. Yes. You amused me. You wanted me to confirm it. It amused me to do so.

Pause.

HARRY. Bill's a slum boy, you see, he's got a slum sense of

humour. That's why I never take him along with me to parties. Because he's got a slum mind. I have nothing against slum minds *per se*, you understand, nothing at all. There's a certain kind of slum mind which is perfectly all right in a slum, but when this kind of slum mind gets out of the slum it sometimes persists, you see, it rots everything. That's what Bill is. There's something faintly putrid about him, don't you find? Like a slug. There's nothing wrong with slugs in their place, but he's a slum slug; there's nothing wrong with slum slugs in their place, but this one won't keep his place – he crawls all over the walls of nice houses, leaving slime, don't you, boy? He confirms stupid sordid little stories just to amuse himself, while everyone else has to run round in circles to get to the root of the matter and smooth the whole thing out. All he can do is sit and suck his bloody hand and decompose like the filthy putrid slum slug he is. What about another whisky, Horne?

JAMES. No, I think I must be off now. Well, I'm glad to hear that nothing did happen. Great relief to me.

HARRY. It must be.

JAMES. My wife's not been very well lately, actually. Overwork.

HARRY. That's bad. Still, you know what it's like in our business.

JAMES. Best thing to do is take her on a long holiday, I think.

HARRY. South of France.

JAMES. The Isles of Greece.

HARRY. Sun's essential, of course.

JAMES. I know. Bermuda.

HARRY. Perfect.

JAMES. Well, thanks very much, Mr. Kane, for clearing my mind. I don't think I'll mention it when I get home. Take her out for a drink or something. Forget all about it.

HARRY. Better hurry up. It's nearly closing time.

JAMES *moves to* BILL, *who is sitting.*

JAMES. I'm very sorry I cut your hand. You're lucky you caught it, of course. Otherwise it might have cut your mouth. Still, it's not too bad, is it?

Pause.

Look . . . I really think I ought to apologize for this silly story my wife made up. The fault is really all hers, and mine, for believing her. You're not to blame for taking it as you did. The whole thing must have been an impossible burden for you. What do you say we shake hands, as a testimony of my goodwill?

JAMES *extends his hand.* BILL *rubs his hand but does not extend it.*

HARRY. Come on, Billy, I think we've had enough of this stupidity, don't you?

Pause.

BILL. I'll . . . tell you . . . the truth.

HARRY. Oh, for God's sake, don't be ridiculous. Come on, Mr. Horne, off you go now, back to your wife, old boy, leave this . . . tyke to me.

JAMES *does not move. He looks down at* BILL.

Come on, Jimmy, I think we've had enough of this stupidity don't you?

JAMES *looks at him sharply.*
HARRY *stops still.*

BILL. I never touched her . . . we sat . . . in the lounge, on a sofa . . . for two hours . . . talked . . . we talked about it . . . we didn't . . . move from the lounge . . . never went to her room . . . just talked . . . about what we would do

. . . if we did get to her room . . . two hours . . . we never touched . . . we just talked about it . . .

Long silence.
JAMES leaves the house.
HARRY sits. BILL remains sitting sucking his hand.
Silence.
Fade house to half light.
Fade up full on flat.
STELLA is lying with the kitten.
The flat door closes. JAMES comes in. He stands looking at her.

JAMES. You didn't do anything, did you?

Pause.

He wasn't in your room. You just talked about it, in the lounge.

Pause.

That's the truth, isn't it?

Pause.

You just sat and talked about what you would do if you went to your room. That's what you did.

Pause.

Didn't you?

Pause.

That's the truth . . . isn't it?

STELLA looks at him, neither confirming nor denying. Her face is friendly, sympathetic.
Fade flat to half light.
The four figures are still, in the half light.
Fade to blackout.

Curtain

The Lover

THE LOVER was first presented by Associated-Rediffusion Television, London, March 28th, 1963, with the following cast:

RICHARD	Alan Badel
SARAH	Vivien Merchant
JOHN	Michael Forrest

Directed by Joan Kemp-Welch

The play was first presented on the stage by Michael Codron and David Hall at the Arts Theatre, September 18th, 1963, with the following cast:

RICHARD	Scott Forbes
SARAH	Vivien Merchant
JOHN	Michael Forrest

Directed by Harold Pinter

Assisted by Guy Vaesen

Summer. A detached house near Windsor

The stage consists of two areas. Living-room right, with small hall and front door up centre. Bedroom and balcony, on a level, left. There is a short flight of stairs to bedroom door. Kitchen off right. A table with a long velvet cover stands against the left wall of the living-room, centre stage. In the small hall there is a cupboard. The furnishings are tasteful, comfortable. (*middle class room*)

SARAH *is emptying and dusting ashtrays in the living-room. It is morning. She wears a crisp, demure dress.* RICHARD *comes into the bedroom from bathroom, off left, collects his briefcase from hall cupboard, goes to* SARAH, *kisses her on the cheek. He looks at her for a moment smiling. She smiles.*

RICHARD (*amiably*). Is your lover coming today?
SARAH. Mmnn.
RICHARD. What time?
SARAH. Three.
RICHARD. Will you be going out . . . or staying in?
SARAH. Oh . . . I think we'll stay in.
RICHARD. I thought you wanted to go to that exhibition.
SARAH. I did, yes . . . but I think I'd prefer to stay in with him today.
RICHARD. Mmn-hmmn. Well, I must be off.

    He goes to the hall and puts on his bowler hat.

RICHARD. Will he be staying long do you think?
SARAH. Mmmmnnn . . .
RICHARD. About . . . six, then.
SARAH. Yes.
RICHARD. Have a pleasant afternoon.
SARAH. Mmnn.
RICHARD. Bye-bye.
SARAH. Bye.

He opens the front door and goes out. She continues dusting.
The lights fade.
Fade up. Early evening. SARAH *comes into room from kitchen.*
She wears the same dress, but is now wearing a pair of very
high-heeled shoes. She pours a drink and sits on chaise longue
with magazine. There are six chimes of the clock. RICHARD
comes in the front door. He wears a sober suit, as in the
morning. He puts his briefcase down in the hall and goes into
the room. She smiles at him and pours him a whisky.

Hullo.

RICHARD. Hullo.

He kisses her on the cheek. Takes glass, hands her the evening
paper and sits down left. She sits on chaise longue with paper.

Thanks.

He drinks, sits back and sighs with contentment.

Aah.

SARAH. Tired?

RICHARD. Just a little.

SARAH. Bad traffic?

RICHARD. No. Quite good traffic, actually.

SARAH. Oh, good.

RICHARD. Very smooth.

Pause.

SARAH. It seemed to me you were just a little late.

RICHARD. Am I?

SARAH. Just a little.

RICHARD. There was a bit of a jam on the bridge.

SARAH gets up, goes to drinks table to collect her glass, sits
again on the chaise longue.

Pleasant day?

SARAH. Mmn. I was in the village this morning.
RICHARD. Oh yes? See anyone?
SARAH. Not really, no. Had lunch.
RICHARD. In the village?
SARAH. Yes.
RICHARD. Any good?
SARAH. Quite fair. (*She sits.*)
RICHARD. What about this afternoon? Pleasant afternoon?
SARAH. Oh yes. Quite marvellous.
RICHARD. Your lover came, did he?
SARAH. Mmnn. Oh yes.
RICHARD. Did you show him the hollyhocks?

   Slight pause.

SARAH. The hollyhocks?
RICHARD. Yes.
SARAH. No, I didn't.
RICHARD. Oh.
SARAH. Should I have done?
RICHARD. No, no. It's simply that I seem to remember your
   saying he was interested in gardening.
SARAH. Mmnn, yes, he is.

   Pause.

   Not all that interested, actually.
RICHARD. Ah.

   Pause.

   Did you go out at all, or did you stay in?
SARAH. We stayed in.
RICHARD. Ah. (*He looks up at the Venetian blinds.*) That blind
   hasn't been put up properly.
SARAH. Yes, it is a bit crooked, isn't it?

   Pause.

RICHARD. Very sunny on the road. Of course, by the time I got on to it the sun was beginning to sink. But I imagine it was quite warm here this afternoon. It was warm in the City.

SARAH. Was it?

RICHARD. Pretty stifling. I imagine it was quite warm everywhere.

SARAH. Quite a high temperature, I believe.

RICHARD. Did it say so on the wireless?

SARAH. I think it did, yes.

Slight pause.

RICHARD. One more before dinner?

SARAH. Mmn.

He pours drinks.

RICHARD. I see you had the Venetian blinds down.

SARAH. We did, yes.

RICHARD. The light was terribly strong.

SARAH. It was. Awfully strong.

RICHARD. The trouble with this room is that it catches the sun so directly, when it's shining. You didn't move to another room?

SARAH. No. We stayed here.

RICHARD. Must have been blinding.

SARAH. It was. That's why we put the blinds down.

Pause.

RICHARD. The thing is it gets so awfully hot in here with the blinds down.

SARAH. Would you say so?

RICHARD. Perhaps not. Perhaps it's just that you feel hotter.

SARAH. Yes. That's probably it.

Pause.

What did you do this afternoon?

RICHARD. Long meeting. Rather inconclusive.

SARAH. It's a cold supper. Do you mind?

RICHARD. Not in the least.

SARAH. I didn't seem to have time to cook anything today.

She moves towards the kitchen.

RICHARD. Oh, by the way . . . I rather wanted to ask you something.

SARAH. What?

RICHARD. Does it ever occur to you that while you're spending the afternoon being unfaithful to me I'm sitting at a desk going through balance sheets and graphs? — *1st hint of Something wrong*

SARAH. What a funny question.

RICHARD. No, I'm curious.

SARAH. You've never asked me that before.

RICHARD. I've always wanted to know.

Slight pause.

SARAH. Well, of course it occurs to me.

RICHARD. Oh, it does?

SARAH. Mmnn.

Slight pause.

RICHARD. What's your attitude to that, then?

SARAH. It makes it all the more piquant. *exciting stimulating*

RICHARD. Does it really?

SARAH. Of course.

RICHARD. You mean while you're with him . . . you actualiy have a picture of me, sitting at my desk going through balance sheets?

SARAH. Only at . . . certain times.

RICHARD. Of course.

SARAH. Not all the time.

RICHARD. Well, naturally.

SARAH. At particular moments.

RICHARD. Mmnn. But, in fact, I'm not completely forgotten?

SARAH. Not by any means.

RICHARD. That's rather touching, I must admit.

Pause.

SARAH. How could I forget you?

RICHARD. Quite easily, I should think.

SARAH. But I'm in your house.

RICHARD. With another.

SARAH. But it's you I love.

RICHARD. I beg your pardon?

SARAH. But it's you I love.

Pause. He looks at her, proffers his glass.

RICHARD. Let's have another drink.

She moves forward. He withdraws his glass, looks at her shoes.

What shoes are they?

SARAH. Mmnn?

RICHARD. Those shoes. They're unfamiliar. Very high-heeled, aren't they?

SARAH (*muttering*). Mistake. Sorry.

RICHARD (*not hearing*). Sorry? I beg your pardon?

SARAH. I'll . . . take them off.

RICHARD. Not quite the most comfortable shoes for an evening at home, I would have thought.

She goes into hall, opens cupboard, puts high-heeled shoes into cupboard, puts on low-heeled shoes. He moves to drinks table, pours himself a drink. She moves to centre table, lights a cigarette.

So you had a picture of me this afternoon, did you, sitting in my office?

SARAH. I did, yes. It wasn't a terribly convincing one, though.

RICHARD. Oh, why not?

SARAH. Because I knew you weren't there. I knew you were with your mistress.

Pause.

RICHARD. Was I?

Short pause.

SARAH. Aren't you hungry?

RICHARD. I had a heavy lunch.

SARAH. How heavy?

He stands at the window.

RICHARD. What a beautiful sunset.

SARAH. Weren't you?

He turns and laughs.

RICHARD. What mistress?

SARAH. Oh, Richard . . .

RICHARD. No, no, it's simply the word that's so odd.

SARAH. Is it? Why?

Slight pause.

I'm honest with you, aren't I? Why can't you be honest with me?

RICHARD. But I haven't got a mistress. I'm very well ac-quainted with a whore, but I haven't got a mistress. There's a world of difference.

SARAH. A whore?

RICHARD (*taking an olive*). Yes. Just a common or garden slut. Not worth talking about. Handy between trains, nothing more.

SARAH. You don't travel by train. You travel by car.

RICHARD. Quite. A quick cup of while cocoa they're checking the oil and water.

Pause.

SARAH. Sounds utterly sterile

RICHARD. No.

Pause.

SARAH. I must say I never expected you to admit it so readily.

RICHARD. Oh, why not? You've never put it to me so bluntly before, have you? Frankness at all costs. Essential to a healthy marriage. Don't you agree?

SARAH. Of course.

RICHARD. You agree.

SARAH. Entirely.

RICHARD. I mean, you're utterly frank with me, aren't you?

SARAH. Utterly.

RICHARD. About your lover. I must follow your example.

SARAH. Thank you.

Pause.

Yes, I have suspected it for some time.

RICHARD. Have you really?

SARAH. Mmnn.

RICHARD. Perceptive.

SARAH. But, quite honestly, I can't really believe she's just . . . what you say.

RICHARD. Why not?

SARAH. It's just not possible. You have such taste. You care so much for grace and elegance in women.

RICHARD. And wit.

SARAH. And wit, yes.

RICHARD. Wit, yes. Terribly important, wit, for a man.

SARAH. Is she witty?

RICHARD (*laughing*). These terms just don't apply. You can't sensibly inquire whether a whore is witty. It's of no significance whether she is or she isn't. She's simply a whore, a functionary who either pleases or displeases.

SARAH. And she pleases you?

RICHARD. Today she is pleasing. Tomorrow . . .? One can't say.

He moves towards the bedroom door taking off his jacket.

SARAH. I must say I find your attitude to women rather alarming.

RICHARD. Why? I wasn't looking for your double, was I? I wasn't looking for a woman I could respect, as you, whom I could admire and love, as I do you. Was I? All I wanted was . . . how shall I put it . . . someone who could express and engender lust with all lust's cunning. Nothing more.

He goes into the bedroom, hangs his jacket up in the ward-robe, and changes into his slippers.
In the living-room SARAH *puts her drink down, hesitates and then follows into the bedroom.*

SARAH. I'm sorry your affair possesses so little dignity.

RICHARD. The dignity is in my marriage.

SARAH. Or sensibility.

RICHARD. The sensibility likewise. I wasn't looking for such attributes. I find them in you.

SARAH. Why did you look at all?

Slight pause.

RICHARD. What did you say?

SARAH. Why look . . . elsewhere . . . at all?

RICHARD. But my dear, you looked. Why shouldn't I look?

Pause.

SARAH. Who looked first?

RICHARD. You.

SARAH. I don't think that's true.

RICHARD. Who, then?

She looks at him with a slight smile.
Fade up. Night. Moonlight on balcony. The lights fade.
RICHARD *comes in bedroom door in his pyjamas. He picks up*
a book and looks at it. SARAH *comes from bathroom in her*
nightdress. There is a double bed. SARAH *sits at the dressing-*
table. Combs her hair.

SARAH. Richard?

RICHARD. Mnn?

SARAH. Do you ever think about me at all . . . when you're
with her?

RICHARD. Oh, a little. Not much.

   Pause.

We talk about you.

SARAH. You talk about me with her?

RICHARD. Occasionally. It amuses her.

SARAH. Amuses her?

RICHARD (*choosing a book*). Mmnn.

SARAH. How . . . do you talk about me?

RICHARD. Delicately. We discuss you as we would play an
antique music box. We play it for our titillation, whenever
desired.

   Pause.

SARAH. I can't pretend the picture gives me great pleasure.

RICHARD. It wasn't intended to. The pleasure is mine.

SARAH. Yes, I see that, of course.

RICHARD (*sitting on the bed*). Surely your own afternoon
pleasures are sufficient for you, aren't they? You don't
expect extra pleasure from my pastimes, do you?

SARAH. No, not at all.

RICHARD. Then why all the questions?

SARAH. Well, it was you who started it. Asking me so many

questions about . . . my side of it. You don't normally do
that.

RICHARD. Objective curiosity, that's all.

He touches her shoulders.

You're not suggesting I'm jealous, surely?

She smiles, stroking his hand.

SARAH. Darling. I know you'd never stoop to that.

RICHARD. Good God, no.

He squeezes her shoulder.

What about you? You're not jealous, are you?

SARAH. No. From what you tell me about your lady I seem to
have a far richer time than you do.

RICHARD. Possibly.

He opens the windows fully and stands by them, looking out.

What peace. Come and look.

She joins him at the window.
They stand silently.

What would happen if I came home early one day, I
wonder?

Pause.

SARAH. What would happen if I followed you one day, I
wonder?

Pause.

RICHARD. Perhaps we could all meet for tea in the village.

SARAH. Why the village? Why not here?

RICHARD. Here? What an extraordinary remark.

Pause.

Your poor lover has never seen the night from this window,
has he?

SARAH. No. He's obliged to leave before sunset, unfortunately.

RICHARD. Doesn't he get a bit bored with these damn afternoons? This eternal teatime? I would. To have as the constant image of your lust a milk jug and teapot. Must be terribly dampening.

SARAH. He's very adaptable. And, of course, when one puts the blinds down it does become a kind of evening.

RICHARD. Yes, I suppose it would.

Pause.

What does he think of your husband?

Slight pause.

SARAH. He respects you.

Pause.

RICHARD. I'm rather moved by that remark, in a strange kind of way. I think I can understand why you like him so much.

SARAH. He's terribly sweet.

RICHARD. Mmn-hmmnn.

SARAH. Has his moods, of course.

RICHARD. Who doesn't?

SARAH. But I must say he's very loving. His whole body emanates love.

RICHARD. How nauseating.

SARAH. No.

RICHARD. Manly with it, I hope?

SARAH. Entirely.

RICHARD. Sounds tedious.

SARAH. Not at all.

Pause.

He has a wonderful sense of humour.

RICHARD. Oh, jolly good. Makes you laugh, does he? Well,

mind the neighbours don't hear you. The last thing we want is gossip.

Pause.

SARAH. It's wonderful to live out here, so far away from the main road, so secluded.

RICHARD. Yes, I do agree.

They go back into the room. They get into the bed. He picks up his book and looks at it. He closes it and puts it down.

This isn't much good.

He switches off his bedside lamp. She does the same. Moonlight.

He's married, isn't he?

SARAH. Mmmmn.

RICHARD. Happily?

SARAH. Mmmmn.

Pause.

And you're happy, aren't you? You're not in any way jealous?

RICHARD. No.

SARAH. Good. Because I think things are beautifully balanced, Richard.

Fade.
Fade up. Morning. SARAH *putting on her negligee in the bedroom. She begins to make the bed.*

SARAH. Darling.

Pause.

Will the shears be ready this morning?

RICHARD (*in bathroom, off*). The what?

SARAH. The shears.
RICHARD. No, not this morning.

He enters, fully dressed in his suit. Kisses her on the cheek.

Not till Friday. Bye-bye.

He leaves the bedroom, collects hat and briefcase from hall.

SARAH. Richard.

He turns.

You won't be home too early today, will you?—
RICHARD. Do you mean he's coming again today? Good
  gracious. He was here yesterday. Coming again today?— *This is*
SARAH. Yes.　　*a signal for another meeting.*
RICHARD. Oh. No, well, I won't be home early. I'll go to the
  National Gallery.
SARAH. Right.
RICHARD. Bye-bye.
SARAH. Bye.

> *The lights fade.*
> *Fade up. Afternoon.* SARAH *comes downstairs into living-
> room. She wears a very tight, low-cut black dress. She hastily
> looks at herself in the mirror. Suddenly notices she is wearing
> low-heeled shoes. She goes quickly to cupboard changes them
> for her high-heeled shoes. Looks again in mirror, smooths her
> hips. Goes to window, pulls venetian blinds down, opens them,
> and closes them until there is a slight slit of light. There are
> three chimes of a clock. She looks at her watch, goes towards
> the flowers on the table. Door bell. She goes to door. It is the
> milkman,* JOHN.

JOHN. Cream?
SARAH. You're very late.
JOHN. Cream?
SARAH. No, thank you.

JOHN. Why not?
SARAH. I have some. Do I owe you anything?
JOHN. Mrs. Owen just had three jars. Clotted.
SARAH. What do I owe you?
JOHN. It's not Saturday yet.
SARAH (*taking the milk*). Thank you.
JOHN. Don't you fancy any cream? Mrs. Owen had three jars.
SARAH. Thank you.

> *She closes the door. Goes into the kitchen with milk. Comes back with a tea-tray, holding teapot and cups, sets it on small table above chaise longue. She briefly attends to the flowers, sits on the chaise longue, crosses her legs, uncrosses them, puts her legs up on chaise longue, smooths her stockings under her skirt. The doorbell rings. Pulling her dress down she moves to the door, opens it.*

Hallo, Max.

> *RICHARD comes in. He is wearing a suede jacket, and no tie. He walks into the room and stands.*
> *She closes the door behind him. Walks slowly down past him, and sits on the chaise longue, crossing her legs.*
> *Pause.*
> *He moves slowly to chaise longue and stands very close to her at her back. She arches her back, uncrosses her legs, moves away to low chair down left.*
> *Pause.*
> *He looks at her, then moves towards the hall cupboard, brings out a bongo drum. He places the drum on the chaise longue, stands.*
> *Pause.*
> *She rises, moves past him towards the hall, turns, looks at him. He moves below chaise. They sit at either end. He begins to tap the drum. Her forefinger moves along drum towards his hand. She scratches the back of his hand sharply. Her hand retreats. Her fingers tap one after the other towards him, and*

[handwritten marginal note: seduction ritual]

rest. Her forefinger scratches between his fingers. Her other
fingers do the same. His legs tauten. His hand clasps hers.
Her hand tries to escape. Wild beats of their fingers tangling.
Stillness.
She gets up, goes to drinks table, lights a cigarette, moves to
window. He puts drum down on chair down right, picks up
cigarette, moves to her.

MAX. Excuse me.

She glances at him and away.

Excuse me, have you got a light?

She does not respond.

Do you happen to have a light?
SARAH. Do you mind leaving me alone?
MAX. Why?

Pause.

I'm merely asking if you can give me a light.

She moves from him and looks up and down the room. He
follows to her shoulder. She turns back.

SARAH. Excuse me.

She moves past him. Close, his body follows.
She stops.

I don't like being followed.
MAX. Just give me a light and I won't bother you. That's all
I want.
SARAH (*through her teeth*). Please go away. I'm waiting for
someone.
MAX. Who?
SARAH. My husband.
MAX. Why are you so shy? Eh? Where's your lighter?

He touches her body. An indrawn breath from her.

Here?

Pause.

Where is it?

He touches her body. A gasp from her.

Here?

She wrenches herself away. He traps her in the corner.

SARAH (*hissing*). What do you think you're doing?
MAX. I'm dying for a puff.
SARAH. I'm waiting for my husband!
MAX. Let me get a light from yours.

> *They struggle silently.*
> *She breaks away to wall.*
> *Silence.*
> *He approaches.*

Are you all right, miss? I've just got rid of that . . . gentle-man. Did he hurt you in any way?
SARAH. Oh, how wonderful of you. No, no, I'm all right. Thank you.
MAX. Very lucky I happened to be passing. You wouldn't believe that could happen in such a beautiful park.
SARAH. No, you wouldn't.
MAX. Still, you've come to no harm.
SARAH. I can never thank you enough. I'm terribly grateful, I really am.
MAX. Why don't you sit down a second and calm yourself.
SARAH. Oh, I'm quite calm – but . . . yes, thank you. You're so kind. Where shall we sit.
MAX. Well, we can't sit out. It's raining. What about that park-keeper's hut?

SARAH. Do you think we should? I mean, what about the park-keeper?

MAX. I am the park-keeper.

They sit on the chaise longue.

SARAH. I never imagined I could meet anyone so kind.

MAX. To treat a lovely young woman like you like that, it's unpardonable.

SARAH (*gazing at him*). You seem so mature, so . . . appreciative.

MAX. Of course.

SARAH. So gentle. So . . . Perhaps it was all for the best.

MAX. What do you mean?

SARAH. So that we could meet. So that we could meet. You and I.

Her fingers trace his thigh. He stares at them, lifts them off.

MAX. I don't quite follow you.

SARAH. Don't you?

Her fingers trace his thigh. He stares at them, lifts them off.

MAX. Now look, I'm sorry. I'm married.

She takes his hand and puts it on her knee.

SARAH. You're so sweet, you mustn't worry.

MAX (*snatching his hand away*). No, I really am. My wife's waiting for me.

SARAH. Can't you speak to strange girls?

MAX. No.

SARAH. Oh, how sickening you are. How tepid.

MAX. I'm sorry.

SARAH. You men are all alike. Give me a cigarette.

MAX. I bloody well won't.

SARAH. I beg your pardon?

MAX. Come here, Dolores.

SARAH. Oh no, not me. Once bitten twice shy, thanks. (*She stands.*) Bye-bye.

MAX. You can't get out, darling. The hut's locked. We're alone. You're trapped.

SARAH. Trapped! I'm a married woman. You can't treat me like this.

MAX (*moving to her*). It's teatime, Mary.

She moves swiftly behind the table and stands there with her back to the wall. He moves to the opposite end of the table, hitches his trousers, bends and begins to crawl under the table towards her.

He disappears under the velvet cloth. Silence. She stares down at the table. Her legs are hidden from view. His hand is on her leg. She looks about, grimaces, grits her teeth, gasps, gradually sinks under the table, and disappears. Long silence.

HER VOICE. Max!

Lights fade.
Fade up.
MAX *sitting on chair down left.*
SARAH *pouring tea.*

SARAH. Max.
MAX. What?
SARAH (*fondly*). Darling.

Slight pause.

What is it? You're very thoughtful.
MAX. No.
SARAH. You are. I know it.

Pause.

MAX. Where's your husband?

Pause.

SARAH. My husband? You know where he is.

MAX. Where?

SARAH. He's at work.

MAX. Poor fellow. Working away, all day.

Pause.

I wonder what he's like.

SARAH (*chuckling*). Oh, Max.

MAX. I wonder if we'd get on. I wonder if we'd . . . you know . . . hit it off.

SARAH. I shouldn't think so.

MAX. Why not?

SARAH. You've got very little in common.

MAX. Have we? He's certainly very accommodating. I mean, he knows perfectly well about these afternoons of ours, doesn't he?

SARAH. Of course.

MAX. He's known for years.

Slight pause.

Why does he put up with it?

SARAH. Why are you suddenly talking about him? I mean what's the point of it? It isn't a subject you normally elaborate on.

MAX. Why does he put up with it?

SARAH. Oh, shut up.

MAX. I asked you a question.

Pause.

SARAH. He doesn't mind.

MAX. Doesn't he?

Slight pause.

Well, I'm beginning to mind.

Pause.

SARAH. What did you say.
MAX. I'm beginning to mind.

Slight pause.

It's got to stop. It can't go on.
SARAH. Are you serious?

Silence.

MAX. It can't go on.
SARAH. You're joking.
MAX. No, I'm not.
SARAH. Why? Because of my husband? Not because of my husband, I hope. That's going a little far, I think.
MAX. No, nothing to do with your husband. It's because of my wife.

Pause.

SARAH. Your wife?
MAX. I can't deceive her any longer.
SARAH. Max . . .
MAX. I've been deceiving her for years. I can't go on with it. It's killing me.
SARAH. But darling, look –
MAX. Don't touch me.

Pause.

SARAH. What did you say?
MAX. You heard.

Pause.

SARAH. But your wife . . . knows. Doesn't she? You've told her . . . all about us. She's known all the time.
MAX. No, she doesn't know. She thinks I know a whore, that's all. Some spare-time whore, that's all. That's what she thinks.

SARAH. Yes, but be sensible . . . my love . . . she doesn't mind, does she?

MAX. She'd mind if she knew the truth, wouldn't she?

SARAH. What truth? What are you talking about?

MAX. She'd mind if she knew that, in fact . . . I've got a full-time mistress, two or three times a week, a woman of grace, elegance, wit, imagination –

SARAH. Yes, yes, you have –

MAX. In an affair that's been going on for years.

SARAH. She doesn't mind, she wouldn't mind – she's happy, she's happy.

Pause.

I wish you'd stop this rubbish, anyway.

She picks up the tea-tray and moves towards the kitchen.

You're doing your best to ruin the whole afternoon.

She takes the tray out. She then returns, looks at MAX and goes to him.

Darling. You don't really think you could have what we have with your wife, do you? I mean, my husband, for instance, completely appreciates that I –

MAX. How does he bear it, your husband? How does he bear it? Doesn't he smell me when he comes back in the evenings? What does he *say*? He must be mad. Now – what's the time – half-past four – now when he's sitting in his office, knowing what's going on here, what does he *feel*, how does he bear it?

SARAH. Max –

MAX. How?

SARAH. He's happy for me. He appreciates the way I am. He understands.

MAX. Perhaps I should meet him and have a word with him.

SARAH. Are you drunk?

MAX. Perhaps I should do that. After all, he's a man, like me. We're both men. You're just a bloody woman.

She slams the table.

SARAH. Stop it! What's the matter with you? What's happened to you? (*Quietly.*) Please, please, stop it. What are you doing, playing a game?

MAX. A game? I don't play games.

SARAH. Don't you? You do. Oh, you do. You do. Usually I like them.

MAX. I've played my last game.

SARAH. Why?

Slight pause.

MAX. The children.

Pause.

SARAH. What?

MAX. The children. I've got to think of the children.

SARAH. What children?

MAX. My children. My wife's children. Any minute now they'll be out of boarding school. I've got to think of them.

She sits close to him.

SARAH. I want to whisper something to you. Listen. Let me whisper to you. Mmmm? Can I? Please? It's whispering time. Earlier it was teatime, wasn't it? Wasn't it? Now it's whispering time.

Pause.

You like me to whisper to you. You like me to love you, whispering. Listen. You mustn't worry about . . . wives, husbands, things like that. It's silly. It's really silly. It's you, you now, here, here with me, here together, that's what it is, isn't it? You whisper to me, you take tea with me, you do that, don't you, that's what we are, that's us, love me.

He stands up.

MAX. You're too bony.

He walks away.

That's what it is, you see. I could put up with everything if it wasn't for that. You're too bony.

SARAH. Me? Bony? Don't be ridiculous.

MAX. I'm not.

SARAH. How can you say I'm bony?

MAX. Every move I make, your bones stick into me. I'm sick and tired of your bones.

SARAH. What are you talking about?

MAX. I'm telling you you're too bony.

SARAH. But I'm fat! Look at me. I'm plump anyway. You always told me I was plump.

MAX. You were plump once. You're not plump any more.

SARAH. Look at me.

He looks.

MAX. You're not plump enough. You're nowhere near plump enough. You know what I like. I like enormous women. Like bullocks with udders. Vast great uddered bullocks.

SARAH. You mean cows.

MAX. I don't mean cows. I mean voluminous great uddered feminine bullocks. Once, years ago, you vaguely resembled one.

SARAH. Oh, thanks.

MAX. But now, quite honestly, compared to my ideal . . .

He stares at her.

. . . you're skin and bone.

They stare at each other.
He puts on his jacket.

SARAH. You're having a lovely joke.
MAX. It's no joke.

He goes out. She looks after him. She turns, goes slowly
towards the bongo drum, picks it up, puts it in the cup-
board. She turns, looks at chaise a moment, walks slowly into
the bedroom, sits on the end of the bed. The lights fade.
Fade up. Early evening. Six chimes of the clock. RICHARD
comes in the front door. He is wearing his sober suit. He puts
his briefcase in cupboard, hat on hook, looks about the room,
pours a drink. SARAH *comes into the bedroom from bathroom,*
wearing a sober dress. They both stand quite still in the two
rooms for a few moments. SARAH *moves to the balcony, looks*
out, RICHARD *comes into the bedroom.*

RICHARD. Hello.

Pause.

SARAH. Hello.
RICHARD. Watching the sunset?

He picks up a bottle.

Drink?
SARAH. Not at the moment, thank you.
RICHARD. Oh, what a dreary conference. Went on all day.
Terribly fatiguing. Still, good work done, I think. Some-
thing achieved. Sorry I'm rather late. Had to have a drink
with one or two of the overseas people. Good chaps.

He sits.

How are you?
SARAH. Fine.

RICHARD. Good.

Silence.

You seem a little depressed. Anything the matter?
SARAH. No.
RICHARD. What sort of day have you had?
SARAH. Not bad.
RICHARD. Not good?

Pause.

SARAH. Fair.
RICHARD. Oh, I'm sorry.

Pause.

Good to be home, I must say. You can't imagine what a comfort it is.

Pause.

Lover come?

She does not reply.

Sarah?
SARAH. What? Sorry. I was thinking of something.
RICHARD. Did your lover come?
SARAH. Oh yes. He came.
RICHARD. In good shape?
SARAH. I have a headache actually.
RICHARD. Wasn't he in good shape?

Pause.

SARAH. We all have our off days.
RICHARD. He, too? I thought the whole point of being a lover is that one didn't. I mean if I, for instance, were called upon to fulfil the function of a lover and felt disposed, shall we say, to accept the job, well, I'd as soon give it up as be found incapable of executing its proper and consistent obligation.

SARAH. You do use long words.

RICHARD. Would you prefer me to use short ones?

SARAH. No, thank you.

Pause.

RICHARD. But I am sorry you had a bad day.

SARAH. It's quite all right.

RICHARD. Perhaps things will improve.

SARAH. Perhaps.

Pause.

I hope so.

She leaves the bedroom, goes into the living-room, lights a cigarette and sits. He follows.

RICHARD. Nevertheless, I find you very beautiful.

SARAH. Thank you.

RICHARD. Yes, I find you very beautiful. I have great pride in being seen with you. When we're out to dinner, or at the theatre.

SARAH. I'm so glad.

RICHARD. Or at the Hunt Ball.

SARAH. Yes, the Hunt Ball.

RICHARD. Great pride, to walk with you as my wife on my arm. To see you smile, laugh, walk, talk, bend, be still. To hear your command of contemporary phraseology, your delicate use of the very latest idiomatic expression, so subtly employed. Yes. To feel the envy of others, their attempts to gain favour with you, by fair means or foul, your austere grace confounding them. And to know you are my wife. It's a source of a profound satisfaction to me.

Pause.

What's for dinner.

SARAH. I haven't thought.

RICHARD. Oh, why not?

SARAH. I find the thought of dinner fatiguing. I prefer not to think about it.

RICHARD. That's rather unfortunate. I'm hungry.

Slight pause.

You hardly expect me to embark on dinner after a day spent sifting matters of high finance in the City.

She laughs.

One could even suggest you were falling down on your wifely duties.

SARAH. Oh dear.

RICHARD. I must say I rather suspected this would happen, sooner or later.

Pause.

SARAH. How's your whore?

RICHARD. Splendid.

SARAH. Fatter or thinner?

RICHARD. I beg your pardon?

SARAH. Is she fatter or thinner?

RICHARD. She gets thinner every day.

SARAH. That must displease you.

RICHARD. Not at all. I'm fond of thin ladies.

SARAH. I thought the contrary.

RICHARD. Really? Why would you have thought that?

Pause.

Of course, your failure to have dinner on the table is quite consistent with the life you've been leading for some time, isn't it?

SARAH. Is it?

RICHARD. Entirely.

Slight pause.

Perhaps I'm being unkind. Am I being unkind?

SARAH (*looks at him*). I don't know.

RICHARD. Yes, I am. In the traffic jam on the bridge just now, you see, I came to a decision.

Pause.

SARAH. Oh? What?

RICHARD. That it has to stop.

SARAH. What?

RICHARD. Your debauchery.

Pause.

Your life of depravity. Your path of illegitimate lust.

SARAH. Really?

RICHARD. Yes, I've come to an irrevocable decision on that point.

She stands.

SARAH. Would you like some cold ham?

RICHARD. Do you understand me?

SARAH. Not at all. I have something cold in the fridge.

RICHARD. Too cold, I'm sure. The fact is this is my house. From today, I forbid you to entertain your lover on these premises. This applies to any time of the day. Is that understood.

SARAH. I've made a salad for you.

RICHARD. Are you drinking?

SARAH. Yes, I'll have one.

RICHARD. What are you drinking?

SARAH. You know what I drink. We've been married ten years.

RICHARD. So we have.

He pours.

It's strange, of course, that it's taken me so long to appreciate the humiliating ignominy of my position.

SARAH. I didn't take my lover ten years ago. Not quite. Not on the honeymoon.

RICHARD. That's irrelevant. The fact is I am a husband who has extended to his wife's lover open house on any afternoon of her desire. I've been too kind. Haven't I been too kind?

SARAH. But of course. You're terribly kind.

RICHARD. Perhaps you would give him my compliments, by letter if you like, and ask him to cease his visits from (*He consults calendar.*) – the twelfth inst.

Long silence.

SARAH. How can you talk like this?

Pause.

Why today . . . so suddenly?

Pause.

Mmmm?

She is close to him.

You've had a hard day . . . at the office. All those overseas people. It's so tiring. But it's silly, it's so silly, to talk like this. I'm here. For you. And you've always appreciated . . . how much these afternoons . . . mean. You've always understood.

She presses her cheek to his.

Understanding is so rare, so dear.

RICHARD. Do you think it's pleasant to know that your wife is unfaithful to you two or three times a week, with great regularity?

SARAH. Richard –

RICHARD. It's insupportable. It has become insupportable. I'm no longer disposed to put up with it.

SARAH (*to him*). Sweet . . . Richard . . . please.

RICHARD. Please what?

She stops.

Can I tell you what I suggest you do?

SARAH. What?

RICHARD. Take him out into the fields. Find a ditch. Or a slag heap. Find a rubbish dump. Mmmm? What about that?

She stands still.

Buy a canoe and find a stagnant pond. Anything. Anywhere. But not my living-room.

SARAH. I'm afraid that's not possible.

RICHARD. Why not?

SARAH. I said it's not possible.

RICHARD. But if you want your lover so much, surely that's the obvious thing to do, since his entry to this house is now barred. I'm trying to be helpful, darling, because of my love for you. You can see that. If I find him on these premises I'll kick his teeth out.

SARAH. You're mad.

He stares at her.

RICHARD. I'll kick his head in.

Pause.

SARAH. What about your own bloody whore?

RICHARD. I've paid her off.

SARAH. Have you? Why?

RICHARD. She was too bony.

Slight pause.

SARAH. But you liked . . . you said you liked . . . Richard
. . . but you love me . . .

RICHARD. Of course.

SARAH. Yes . . . you love me . . . you don't mind him . . .
you understand him . . . don't you ? . . . I mean, you know
better than I do . . . darling . . . all's well . . . all's well
. . . the evenings . . . and the afternoons . . . do you see ?
Listen, I do have dinner for you. It's ready. I wasn't serious.
It's Boeuf bourgignon. And tomorrow I'll have Chicken
Chasseur. Would you like it ?

They look at each other.

RICHARD (*softly*). Adulteress.

SARAH. You can't talk like this, it's impossible, you know you
can't. What do you think you're doing ?

*He remains looking at her for a second, then moves into the
hall.*
He opens the hall cupboard and takes out the bongo drum.
She watches him.
He returns.

RICHARD. What's this ? I found it some time ago. What is it ?

Pause.

What is it ?

SARAH. You shouldn't touch that.

RICHARD. But it's in my house. It belongs either to me, or to
you, or to another.

SARAH. It's nothing. I bought it in a jumble sale. It's nothing.
What do you think it is ? Put it back.

RICHARD. Nothing ? This ? A drum in my cupboard ?

SARAH. Put it back!

RICHARD. It isn't by any chance anything to do with your
illicit afternoons ?

SARAH. Not at all. Why should it?

RICHARD. It is used. This is used, isn't it? I can guess.

SARAH. You guess nothing. Give it to me.

RICHARD. How does he use it? How do you use it? Do you
play it while I'm at the office?

*She tries to take the drum. He holds on to it. They are still,
hands on the drum.*

What function does this fulfil? It's not just an ornament, I
take it? What do you do with it?

SARAH (*with quiet anguish*). You've no right to question me.
No right at all. It was our arrangement. No questions of this
kind. Please. Don't, don't. It was our arrangement.

RICHARD. I want to know.

She closes her eyes.

SARAH. Don't . . .

RICHARD. Do you both play it? Mmmmnn? Do you both
play it? Together?

She moves away swiftly, then turns, hissing.

SARAH. You stupid . . .! (*She looks at him coolly.*) Do you think
he's the only one who comes! Do you? Do you think he's the
only one I entertain? Mmmnn? Don't be silly. I have other
visitors, other visitors, all the time, I receive all the time.
Other afternoons, all the time. When neither of you know,
neither of you. I give them strawberries in season. With
cream. Strangers, total strangers. But not to me, not while
they're here. They come to see the hollyhocks. And then they
stay for tea. Always. Always.

RICHARD. Is that so?

*He moves towards her, tapping the drum gently.
He faces her, tapping, then grasps her hand and scratches it
across the drum.*

SARAH. What are you doing?
RICHARD. Is that what you do?

reverb
to being
mat.

> *She jerks away, to behind the table.*
> *He moves towards her, tapping.*

Like that?

> *Pause.*

What fun.

> *He scratches the drum sharply and then places it on the chair.*

Got a light?

> *Pause.*

Got a light?

> *She retreats towards the table, eventually ending behind it.*

Come on, don't be a spoilsport. Your husband won't mind, if you give me a light. You look a little pale. Why are you so pale? A lovely girl like you.
SARAH. Don't, don't say that!
RICHARD. You're trapped. We're alone. I've locked up.
SARAH. You mustn't do this, you mustn't do it, you mustn't!
RICHARD. He won't mind.

> *He begins to move slowly closer to the table.*

No one else knows.

> *Pause.*

No one else can hear us. No one knows we're here.

> *Pause.*

Come on. Give us a light.

Pause.

You can't get out, darling. You're trapped.

They face each other from opposite ends of the table.
She suddenly giggles.
Silence.

SARAH. I'm trapped.

Pause.

What will my husband say?

Pause.

He expects me. He's waiting. I can't get out. I'm trapped. You've no right to treat a married woman like this. Have you? Think, think, think of what you're doing.

She looks at him, bends and begins to crawl under the table towards him. She emerges from under the table and kneels at his feet, looking up. Her hand goes up his leg. He is looking down at her.

You're very forward. You really are. Oh, you really are. But my husband will understand. My husband does understand. Come here. Come down here. I'll explain. After all, think of my marriage. He adores me. Come here and I'll whisper to you. I'll whisper it. It's whispering time. Isn't it?

She takes his hands. He sinks to his knees, with her. They are kneeling together, close. She strokes his face.

It's a very late tea. Isn't it? But I think I like it. Aren't you sweet? I've never seen you before after sunset. My husband's at a late-night conference. Yes, you look different. Why are you wearing this strange suit, and this tie? You usually wear something else, don't you? Take off your jacket. Mmmnn? Would you like me to change? Would you like me to change my clothes? I'll change for you, darling. Shall I? Would you like that?

Silence. She is very close to him.

RICHARD. Yes.

Pause.

Change.

Pause.

Change.

Pause.

Change your clothes.

Pause.

You lovely whore.

They are still, kneeling, she leaning over him.

THE END

The Examination

The Examination

When we began, I allowed him intervals. He expressed no desire for these, nor any objection. And so I took it upon myself to adjudge their allotment and duration. They were not consistent, but took alteration with what I must call the progress of our talks. With the chalk I kept I marked the proposed times upon the blackboard, before the beginning of a session, for him to examine, and to offer any criticism if he felt so moved. But he made no objection, nor, during our talks, expressed any desire for a break in the proceedings. However, as I suspected they might benefit both of us, I allowed him intervals.

The intervals themselves, when they occurred, at whatever juncture, at whatever crucial point, preceded by whatever deadlock, were passed, naturally, in silence. It was not uncommon for them to be both preceded and followed by an equal silence, but this is not to say that on such occasions their purpose was offended. Frequently his disposition would be such that little could be achieved by insistence, or by persuasion. When Kullus was disposed to silence I invariably acquiesced, and prided myself on those occasions with tactical acumen. But I did not regard these silences as intervals, for they were not, and neither, I think, did Kullus so regard them. For if Kullus fell silent, he did not cease to participate in our examination. Never, at any time, had I reason to doubt his active participation, through word and through silence, between interval and interval, and I recognized what I took to be his devotion as actual and unequivocal, besides, as it seemed to me, obligatory. And so the nature of our silence within the frame of our examination, and the nature of our silence outside the frame of our examination, were entirely opposed.

Upon my announcement of an interval Kullus would change, or act in such a manner as would suggest change. His behaviour, on these occasions, was not consistent, nor, I am convinced, was it initiated by motives of resentment or enmity, although I suspect Kullus was aware of my watchfulness. Not that I made any pretence to be otherwise. I was obliged to remark, and, if possible, to verify, any ostensible change in his manner, whether it was outside the frame of our examination or not. And it is upon this point that I could be accused of error. For gradually it appeared that these intervals proceeded according to his terms. And where both allotment and duration had rested with me, and had become my imposition, they now proceeded according to his dictates, and became his imposition.

For he journeyed from silence to silence, and I had no course but to follow. Kullus's silence, where he was entitled to silence, was compounded of numerous characteristics, the which I duly noted. But I could not always follow his courses, and where I could not follow, I was no longer his dominant.

Kullus's predilection for windows was not assumed. At every interval, he retired to the window, and began from its vantage, as from a source. On approaching initially when the break was stated, he paid no attention to the aspect beyond, either in day-time or in night-time. And only in his automatic course to the window, and his lack of interest in the aspect beyond, did he prove consistent.

Neither was Kullus's predilection for windows a deviation from former times. I had myself suffered under his preoccupation upon previous occasions, when the order of his room had been maintained by particular arrangement of window and curtain, according to day and to night, and seldom to my taste or my comfort. But now he maintained no such order and did not determine their opening or closing. For we were no longer in Kullus's room.

And the window was always open, and the curtains were always open.

Not that Kullus displayed any interest in this constant

arrangement, in the intervals, when he might note it. But as I suspect he was aware of my watchfulness, so I suspect he was aware of my arrangement. Dependent on the intensity of his silence I could suspect and conclude, but where his silence was too deep for echo, I could neither suspect nor conclude. And so gradually, where this occurred, I began to take the only course open to me, and terminated the intervals arbitrarily, cutting short the proposed duration, when I could no longer follow him, and was no longer his dominant.

But this was not until later.

When the door opened. When Kullus, unattended, entered, and the interim ended. I turned from all light in the window, to pay him due regard and welcome. Whereupon without reserve or hesitation, he moved from the door as from shelter, and stood in the light from the window. So I watched the entrance become vacant, which had been his shelter. And observed the man I had welcomed, he having crossed my border.

Equally, now, I observed the selected properties, each in their place; the blackboard, the window, the stool. And the door had closed and was absent, and of no moment. Imminent upon opening and welcoming it had possessed moment. Now only one area was to witness activity and to suffer procedure, and that only was necessary and valid. For the door was closed and so closed.

Whereupon I offered Kullus the stool, the which I placed for him. He showed, at this early juncture, no disregard for my directions; if he did not so much obey, he extended his voluntary co-operation. This was sufficient for my requirements. That I detected in him a desire for a summation of our efforts spoke well for the progress of our examination. It was my aim to avoid the appearance of subjection; a common policy, I understand, in like examinations. Yet I was naturally dominant, by virtue of my owning the room; he having entered through the door I now closed. To be confronted with the

especial properties of my abode, bearing the seal and arrangement of their tenant, allowed only for recognition on the part
of my visitor, and through recognition to acknowledgement
and through acknowledgement to appreciation, and through
appreciation to subservience. At least, I trusted that such a
development would take place, and initially believed it to have
done so. It must be said, however, that his manner, from time
to time, seemed to border upon indifference, yet I was not
deluded by this, or offended. I viewed it as a utility he was
compelled, and entitled, to fall back on, and equally as a tribute
to my own incisiveness and patience. And if then I viewed it
as a tactical measure, it caused me little concern. For it seemed,
at this time, that the advantage was mine. Had not Kullus
been obliged to attend this examination? And was not his
attendance an admission of that obligation? And was not his
admission an acknowledgement of my position? And my position therefore a position of dominance? I calculated this to be
so, and no early event caused me to re-assess this calculation.
Indeed, so confident was I in the outcome of our talks, that I
decided to allow him intervals.

To institute these periods seemed to me both charitable and
politic. For I hoped he might benefit from a period of no
demand, so be better equipped for the periods of increased
demand which would follow. And, for a time, I had no reason
to doubt the wisdom of this arrangement. Also, the context
of the room in which Kullus moved during the intervals was
familiar and sympathetic to me, and not so to him. For Kullus
had known it, and now knew it no longer, and took his place
in it as a stranger, and when each break was stated, was compelled to pursue a particular convention and habit in his
course, so as not to become hopelessly estranged within its
boundaries. But gradually it became apparent that only in his
automatic course to the window, and his lack of interest in the
aspect beyond, did he prove consistent.

Prior to his arrival, I had omitted to establish one property

in the room, which I knew to be familiar to him, and so liable
to bring him ease. And never once did he remark the absence
of a flame in the grate. I concluded he did not recognize this
absence. To balance this, I emphasized the presence of the
stool, indeed, placed it for him, but as he never once remarked
this presence, I concluded his concern did not embrace it.
Not that it was at any time simple to determine by what
particular his concern might be engaged. However, in the
intervals, when I was able to observe him with possibly a finer
detachment, I hoped to determine this.

Until his inconsistency began to cause me alarm, and his
silence to confound me.

I can only assume Kullus was aware, on these occasions, of
the scrutiny of which he was the object, and was persuaded to
resist it, and to act against it. He did so by deepening the
intensity of his silence, and by taking courses I could by no
means follow, so that I remained isolated, and outside his
silence, and thus of negligible influence. And so I took the
only course open to me, and terminated the intervals arbitrarily, cutting short the proposed duration, when I could no
longer follow him, and was no longer his dominant.

For where the intervals had been my imposition, they had
now become his imposition.

Kullus made no objection to this adjustment, though without doubt he noted my anxiety. For I suffered anxiety with
good cause, out of concern for the progress of our talks, which
now seemed to me to be affected. I was no longer certain
whether Kullus participated in our examination, nor certain
whether he still understood that as being the object of our
meeting. Equally, the nature of our silences, which formerly
were distinct in their opposition: that is, a silence within the
frame of our examination, and a silence outside the frame of
our examination; seemed to me no longer opposed, indeed
were indistinguishable, and were one silence, dictated by
Kullus.

And so the time came when Kullus initiated intervals at his own inclination, and pursued his courses at will, and I was able to remark some consistency in his behaviour. For now I followed him in his courses without difficulty, and there was no especial duration for interval or examination, but one duration, in which I participated. My devotion was actual and unequivocal. I extended my voluntary co-operation, and made no objection to procedure. For I desired a summation of our efforts. And when Kullus remarked the absence of a flame in the gate, I was bound to acknowledge this. And when he remarked the presence of the stool, I was equally bound. And when he removed the blackboard, I offered no criticism. And when he closed the curtains I did not object.

For we were now in Kullus's room.

Methuen's Modern Plays

EDITED BY JOHN CULLEN

Heinar Kipphardt *In the Matter of J. Robert*
                  Oppenheimer
Arthur Kopit   *Oh Dad, Poor Dad*
Henry Livings   *Kelly's Eye and other plays*
                  Eh?
John Mortimer   *Two Stars for Comfort*
                  The Judge
Joe Orton   *Loot*
                  Crimes of Passion
Harold Pinter   *The Birthday Party*
                  The Room and The Dumb Waiter
                  The Caretaker
                  A Slight Ache and other plays
                  The Collection and The Lover
                  The Homecoming
                  Tea Party and other plays
Jean-Paul Sartre *Crime Passionel*
Theatre Workshop *Oh What a Lovely War*
and Charles Chilton

*   *   *

Methuen's Theatre Classics

THE TROJAN WOMEN   Euripides
                   an English Version by
                   Neil Curry
THE REDEMPTION   *Adapted by Gordon*
                   Honeycombe from five
                   cycles of Mystery Plays
THE MISANTHROPE   Moliere
                   translated by
                   Richard Wilbur
IRONHAND   Goethe
                   adapted by John Arden

THE GOVERNMENT INSPECTOR	Gogol *an English version by* *Edward O. Marsh and* *Jeremy Brooks*
BRAND	Ibsen
THE WILD DUCK	*translated by Michael Meyer*
HEDDA GABLER	
THE MASTER BUILDER	
MISS JULIE	Strindberg *translated by Michael Meyer*
LADY WINDERMERE'S FAN	Wilde
THE IMPORTANCE OF BEING EARNEST	
THE PLAYBOY OF THE WESTERN WORLD	Synge

*   *   *

Methuen Playscripts

Paul Ableman	*Tests*
Barry Bermange	*Nathan and Tabileth* and *Oldenberg*
Edward Bond	*Saved*
Kenneth H. Brown	*The Brig*
David Campton	*Little Brother: Little Sister* and *Out of the Flying Pan*
Henry Chapman	*You Won't Always be on Top*
David Cregan	*Three Men for Colverton* *Transcending* and *The Dancers*
John McGrath	*Events While Guarding the Bofor's Gun*
Georges Michel	*The Sunday Walk*
Rodney Milgate	*A Refined Look at Existence*
Guillaume Oyono-Mbia	*Three Suitors: One Husband* and *Until Further Notice*

Other Plays from Methuen